'STACHE

FRIVOLOUS FACTS & FANCIES

'STACHE

ABOUT THAT SPACE BETWEEN
THE NOSE AND LIP

Terry Taylor

LARK CRAFTS

A Division of
Sterling Publishing Co., Inc.
New York / London

Editor: Larry Shea
Editorial Assistant: Meagan Shirlen
Art Directors: Shannon Yokeley & Chris Bryant
Illustrations: Orrin Lundgren
Photographer: Steve Mann
Interior & Cover Designer: Travis Medford

10 9 8 7 6 5 4 3 2 1

First Edition

Published by Lark Books, A Division of
Sterling Publishing Co., Inc.
387 Park Avenue South, New York, NY 10016

Distributed in Canada by Sterling Publishing,
c/o Canadian Manda Group, 165 Dufferin Street
Toronto, Ontario, Canada M6K 3H6

Distributed in the United Kingdom
by GMC Distribution Services,
Castle Place, 166 High Street, Lewes,
East Sussex, England BN7 1XU

Distributed in Australia by Capricorn Link (Australia) Pty Ltd.,
P.O. Box 704, Windsor, NSW 2756 Australia

If you have questions or comments about this book, please contact:
Lark Books, 67 Broadway, Asheville, NC 28801
828-253-0467

Manufactured in China

ISBN 13: 978-1-60059-625-4

For information about custom editions, special sales, premium
and corporate purchases, please contact Sterling Special Sales
Department at 800-805-5489 or specialsales@sterlingpub.com.

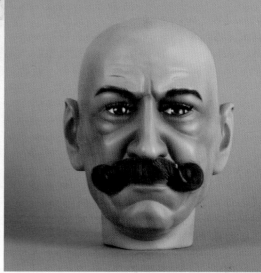

CONTENTS

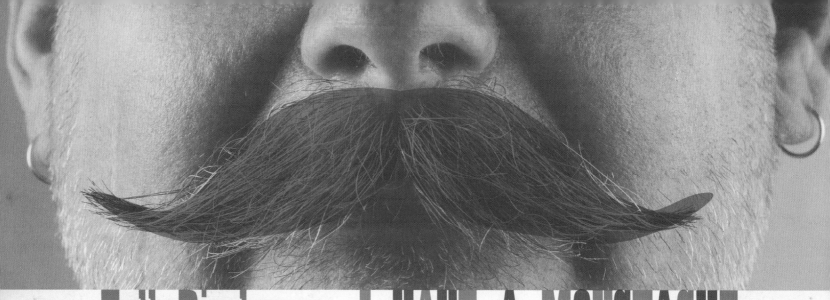

Full Disclosure: I HAVE A MOUSTACHE.

In the mid-1970s I grew a mustache—do the math, if you must. Later I paired it with stubbly cheeks and continued to wear it that way until the turn of the 21st century. It was a neatly trimmed but unremarkable 'stache, until just a couple of years ago.

I don't know what came over me. Let's just say I got an itch under my lip. Tom, my trusty barber, has tended to my tonsorial needs for 20 years. (An ever-growing bald spot and touches of silver make a bi-weekly buzz cut a must.) One day I stopped Tom from trimming my mustache and told him I'd been thinking of trying something different. Tom wisely proffered, "Go ahead; you can always cut it off if you don't like it."

Now, many purists insist that a moustache—like the cheese—must stand alone; unaccompanied by extraneous whiskers of any kind.

No closely clipped cheeks, goatees, or soul patches allowed. Purists be damned! Here's where I stand: if the fuzz on the lip is prominently displayed, it's a 'stache.

Let's hear it for creative whiskering! A jaunty handlebar isn't anachronistic; the lush Franz Joseph is back in style after a long hiatus. Even that German dictator's style of 'stache isn't the mark of whiskery shame it once was. Be bold (and patient) if you want a mustache. Braid it. Dye it (if you dare). Grow it, cut it off, and then sell it on eBay! Really. But don't let anything stop you from moving your inner 'stache to the upper lip where it belongs.

Perhaps you've noticed the upper lips of the famous on the covers of glossy weekly magazines.

Do you know any guys who've just returned from extended vacations or noticed the stiff upper lips that accompany mid-life crises? What do they all have in common?—an incipient or fully realized mustache!

If you're in a hurry to stachify your lip, your best bet is to go faux (unless you're blessed with a one-o'clock shadow). Get crafty: stitch, paint, draw, fold, quill, or carve a moustache for yourself. You can whip one up in way-less-than-an-hour, just in time for an interminable staff meeting or a dreaded blind date.

And why should your upper lip draw all the attention? Wear a 'stache on a t-shirt, send one in the mail, or stitch one to a sock monkey! Crafters everywhere are adorning almost any and

every thing imaginable with mustaches. Support those creative online and local crafters who are making such great stuff. Or d-i-y some yourself. It's not rocket science.

In this little book you'll find a hirsute history of the moustache since the dawn of time, the good works 'staches accomplish, and other fuzzy information. You'll think up uses for the 'stache-y stickers to astound your friends and, perhaps, your foes. Get creative with them. Make a faux 'stache if you need one or grow a real one. After all, you can always shave it off.

'Stache away.

9

A Hirsute History of the 'Stache

Did Adam have a mustache? Early cavemen? Perhaps, if they could bear shaving off their beards with sharpened flint or stone razors. What about King Tutankhamen? His royal barber would have shaved him with a copper or bronze razor. But what about that "beard" on Tut's golden mummy mask? It may have been a false beard that marked him as a living god. Even Queen Hatsheput was depicted in royal portraits with the same sort of narrow false beard.

Alexander the Great had a penchant for not appearing in battles with a beard, so the Greeks are mostly portrayed in sculpture as clean-shaven, except for philosophers, it appears. The Romans followed suit: Julius Caesar had his whiskers plucked. The shaved face was "in," until around the time of Hadrian's rule (117–138 CE). He was the first Roman Emperor pictured in sculpture with a beard.

China's First Emperor, Qin Shihuangdi, commissioned a terra cotta army to accompany him in his vast burial tomb. Ranks of soldiers appeared in all their mustached glory. If they *had* shaved, bronze razors would have been used to shave their chins and cheeks.

For many centuries, the rich and powerful of Europe were set apart from their servants and the lower classes by their

hairless faces. The rich could afford to have their beards styled or whiskers selectively shaved to create mustaches. After all, they didn't have to scramble for their living. Soon mustaches and beards became the marks of indolence, style, and sometimes power.

In France, during the 1400s, King Charles VII was pictured with such a trim mustache that it almost appears penciled in. Henry VIII in England had a very trim beard and mustache as well. In the 1600s, paintings of Charles II of England and Ludovic XIV of France show them with neat mustaches. Neatly manicured 'staches were stylish in the 17th century, paired with extravagantly curled wigs. Unlike most clerics of that period, popes Pius V and Innocent X sported full beards with mustaches.

During the 1700s, mustaches and beards fell out of style, except for the bold mustache worn by Peter the Great of Russia. The powdered perukes and periwigs of 18th century were seldom—if ever—paired with facial hair. It just wasn't done.

The moustache came into its own in a big way during the 19th century. In Europe, the craze for mustaches began in the military ranks of France, Prussia, and the British hussars. For some in the military, mustaches were required wearing! Franz Joseph I, Emperor of Austria, King of Bohemia, and King of Hungary inspired men to wear long side-whiskers that merged with a bushy mustache for a formidable look called—you guessed it—the Franz Joseph. In 1838, the emperor issued an ordinance specifically forbidding civilians to wear moustaches. He commanded police and other authorities to arrest and shave anyone who dared wear one. In France, Napoleon III wore a regal goatee topped with a heavily waxed moustache, the ends tightly twirled into sharp points. That style was known as the Imperial.

In early photographs from the American Civil War era you see a great many soldiers wearing facial hair of all types.

Was it because there was little access to shaving time? During that conflict, General George McClellan wore a mustache. Many other generals wore full beards with mustaches. I have family pictures of my great-great-great grandfather, a physician during the Civil War, wearing a mustache well after the war was over. His son did, too. Check your own family tree and I'll bet you find some 'staches.

Other notables sporting bushy 'staches include Mark Twain and Colonel W.F. Cody, otherwise known as Buffalo Bill. He traveled around the world with his famous show Wild West and Congress of Rough Riders of the World. Three American presidents of that era—Ulysses S. Grant, Rutherford B. Hayes, and James Garfield—wore full beards. Chester A. Arthur, Grover Cleveland, and Theodore Roosevelt proudly wore bold, solo mustaches in the 1800s. William H. Taft has the singular honor of being the sole United States President of the 20th century to wear a moustache.

In the early 20th century, mustaches became much more sedate in appearance. In the U.S., popular opinion held that mustaches were worn only by foreigners and immigrants. Unless a film star was playing a villain, a 'stache was rarely worn. Charlie Chaplin's little toothbrush 'stache from the era of silent films was an exception. Yes, a few box office stars, such

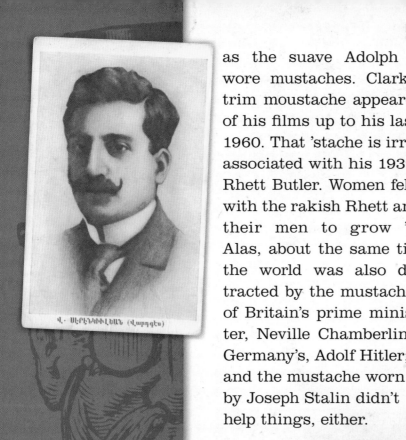

Վ. ՍԵՐԵՆԿԻՒԼԵԱՆ (վարդզես)

as the suave Adolph Menjou, wore mustaches. Clark Gable's trim moustache appeared in all of his films up to his last one in 1960. That 'stache is irrevocably associated with his 1939 role as Rhett Butler. Women fell in love with the rakish Rhett and urged their men to grow 'staches. Alas, about the same time, the world was also distracted by the mustaches of Britain's prime minister, Neville Chamberlin; Germany's, Adolf Hitler; and the mustache worn by Joseph Stalin didn't help things, either.

It's no wonder that mustaches sort of disappeared in the 1950s after the bad rap they had achieved up to and during the Second World War. In the 1950s, a renaissance of imagery from the late-Victorian period of the 19th century—a.k.a. the Gay Nineties—was used in design motifs on cocktail glasses, greeting cards, and more.

The GAY NINETIES MUSTACHE

MAKES EM LAUGH

WYATT EARP   RENE DESCARTES   GUSTAVE FLAUBERT   ELIHU ROOT   DENNIS WEAVER

Inevitably, the motifs featured men dressed in vests, striped shirts, and armbands sporting bold, black handlebars. Around the same time there was a revival of interest in rag-time music—think banjos and player-piano rolls—that gave birth to establishments as Your Father's Mustache in Boston and New York City, and Goman's Gay Nineties in San Francisco.

Only a few mustaches from the 1950s appeared on the tiny, black-and-white television screen. First—dear to the hearts of millions of tots—was the marvelous mustache of Captain Kangaroo. Dressed in his coat with the huge pockets that held marvelous things, there was absolutely nothing scary about the Captain's walrus 'stache. However, as a kid I found Groucho Marx kind of scary. Very early in his career, Groucho wore bold eyebrows and a mustache created with boot blacking or stage makeup as he and his zany brothers cavorted on the silver screen. When Groucho made the transition from film to television, he grew a real 'stache. Even the wacky-look-ing duck that descended from above whenever a contestant spoke the secret word wore a black 'stache and glasses.

YOUR FATHER'S
Mustache

BOSTON
NEW YORK
CAPE COD

74 Warrington St.
125 Seventh Ave. So.
Route 24   Harwich

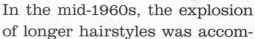

In the mid-1960s, the explosion of longer hairstyles was accompanied by a revival of the art of growing mustaches. George Harrison of The Beatles returned from a trip to India wearing a kurta *and* a mustache. At the end of 1966, John, Paul, and Ringo grew mustaches, too. All four of the fab ones were photographed wearing 'staches on the cover of *Sgt. Pepper's Lonely Hearts Club Band* in 1967. Paul shaved his off soon after the album's release, but Ringo's 'stache has more or less been intact since then. Is it any surprise that mustaches became *de riguer* for at least one member of any rock and roll band? Think David Crosby of Crosby, Stills, Nash and Young; Jimi Hendrix; Carlos Santana; and almost anyone who performed at Woodstock (except for Janis Joplin). You get the picture.

The tastefully nude centerfold of the mustachioed (and hirsute) Burt Reynolds that appeared in the April, 1972, issue of *Cosmopolitan* magazine set the tone for the 1970s. For the four-season run of *Welcome Back, Kotter*, Gabe Kaplan's head of curls was complemented by his full mustache. Several members of the Village People (and untold numbers of gay men

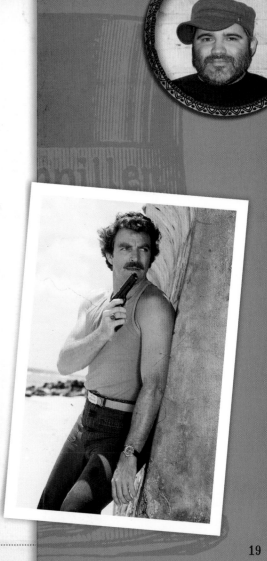

dancing to the disco beat in flannel shirts) wore 'staches. The great Oakland A's relief pitcher Rollie Fingers grew his signature curled-tip 'stache in the 1970s. That decade was a 'stache-fest, culminating in the series debut of *Magnum, P.I.* in 1980.

Face it: Tom Selleck's and John Hillerman's mustaches were the perfect storm of mustacheness. Hall and Oates' four top-ten singles of 1981 and John Oates' moustache were nothing compared to Magnum P.I.'s lush 'stache. Every man who could grow one had to have one. Mustaches were more popular than mullets (thankfully). But nothing lasts forever. By the end of the decade, except for occasional sightings on Boston Red Sox' Wade Boggs and the divine John Waters, the heyday of the 'stache had been trimmed back. Considerably.

So far, in the first years of the 21st century, moustaches are making a definite comeback. Men are more willing to experiment with facial hair in their quest to make a unique statement. More flamboyant mustaches—'staches that baroquely flow and curl—are making an appearance once again. The closely-cropped, pencil-thin mustache is back. Mutton chops, Fu Manchus, goatees, soul patches, and more are not uncommon. There's hope for the future.

'STACHES OF THE SILVER SCREEN

Clark Gable didn't give a damn: he kept his neatly trimmed moustache until the very end of his career.

Best known for his character "The Tramp," **Charlie Chaplin**'s Hitlerian turn in *The Great Dictator* is hilarious.

Cheech Marin sported the moustache; Tommy Chong grew the beard. Got that straight?

John Waters' pencil-thin moustache is—to put it frankly, my dears—divine.

When he first appeared with his brothers Zeppo, Harpo, and Chico, **Groucho Marx**'s moustache was faux: painted on with greasepaint!

Posed on a bearskin rug in a famous 1972 *Cosmopolitan* magazine centerfold, **Burt Reynolds** proudly displayed his mustache to millions of adoring readers.

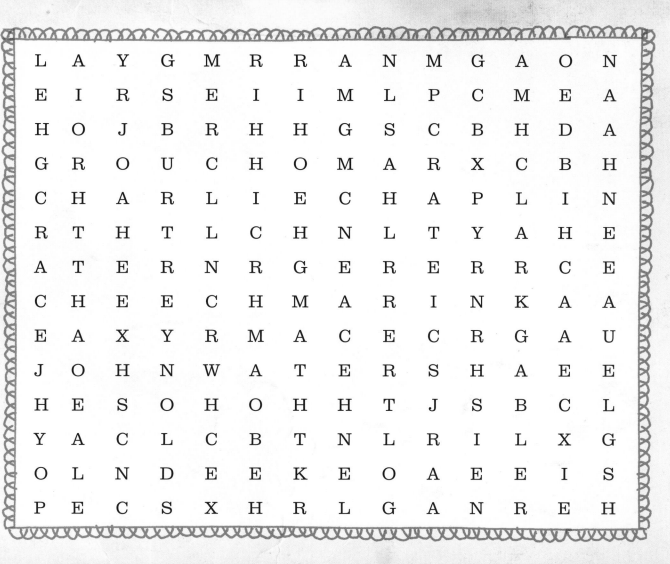

```
L A Y G M R R A N M G A O N
E I R S E I I M L P C M E A
H O J B R H H G S C B H D A
G R O U C H O M A R X C B H
C H A R L I E C H A P L I N
R T H T L C N L T Y A H E
A T E R N R G E R E R R C E
C H E E C H M A R I N K A A
E A X Y R M A C E C R G A U
J O H N W A T E R S H A E E
H E S O H O H H T J S B C L
Y A C L C B T N L R I L X G
O L N D E E K E O A E E I S
P E C S X H R L G A N R E H
```

The Art & Craft of the Mustache

Aside from Salvador Dali's elegant moustache (a work of art in its own right), the most famous work of mustache art has to be the one created by Marcel Duchamp in 1919. Marcel drew a 'stache and a goatee on the Mona Lisa. Oh yes, he did. But Marcel didn't sneak into the Louvre one dark and stormy night to pencil one in on the canvas. He simply bought a postcard, sketched on a mustache, and wrote a cryptic L.H.O.O.Q. along the bottom edge. Is it art? Of course it is. (If you want to know what it means, read an art history book. This book is about the 'stache.)

Does the idea of adding a mustache to the Mona Lisa tickle your funny bone? It tickled mine. And I'd like to imagine that Monsieur Duchamp wouldn't mind if I made my very own versions. So I did (and you can too). Use press-on lettering (commas and parentheses are my favorites), marking pens, or the 'stache stickers. Imagine what a 'stache would look like on Whistler's mother, Grant Wood's farm couple in American Gothic, or Gilbert Stuart's portrait of George Washington.

Have you noticed the flurry of mustaches popping up on the darnedest things? Indie crafters are adorning stuffed animals, t-shirts, and pillows; letterpress and print shops are in love with the handlebar; jewelers, woodworkers, and potters are turning out 'staches of all shapes and sizes. There's a tsunami of 'staches at online sites such as Etsy.

Throughout this book I've sprinkled some 'stache stuff to inspire your crafty side. Make your own mustaches to wear; add a 'stache or two to a baseball cap or a pair of boxers. Use your imagination and tickle someone's funny bone.

THE MOUSTACHE

HOW TO:

GLUE

YOU RULE.

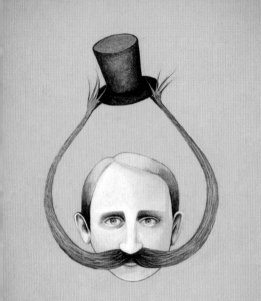

MUST-ACHIO

NUT!

WANT
TO . RIDE . ON . MY
HANDLE-
BARS ?

FUZZY
'STACHE

AH, the versatile chenille stem. If you haven't twisted and fiddled with "pipe cleaners" since you were a kid at camp, you'll discover a rainbow of colors to play with at your local craft store. Coordinate the mo' with your outfit!

1 Fold the stem in half. Turn the stem so the fold is pointing down and the free legs are pointing up.

2 Make an M shape, with the long legs pointing down alongside the first fold.

3 Now style your moustache. Twirl the ends into tight curls, whoosh the ends up, or bend them down wavily into a Fu Manchu

4 Insert the M into your nostrils and adjust the fit. It will tickle a bit, but no matter how close you are, don't let a friend wear this moustache! Show him or her how to make one.

Top 10 Reasons You Might Want to Grow a Moustache

1 You're running from the law. (It's quicker to shave one off than to grow one after the fact.)

2 You're tired of looking at the same face in the mirror. (You might want to consider other alternatives if you're a woman).

3 You want to join a biker gang. (That banana-seat bicycle isn't going to cut it.)

4 You want to irritate your spouse. (Careful now: divorce is an expensive process.)

5 A bushy one might make an excellent hiding place. (Note to self: limit the size of your stolen items).

6 You want to tickle someone's fancy. (Interpret this one any way you wish!)

7 You're underage and you want to look older. (They'll still card you.)

Your upper lip is cold. (That lip sweater grandma knit you for Christmas really itches.)

Your walrus spirit guide told you to. (Sounds better than saying your kitty cat told you to do it.)

All the cool kids are doing it. (What more do you need?)

So You Want to Grow a Moustache?

Here's a fact for you: the average rate of growth for human body hair is approximately ½ inch (1.3 cm) per month. Before you start wondering why you don't look like a yeti, you should know that your genes (not jeans) determine how thickly hair follicles are distributed on your body. For men and women alike, heredity determines maximum lengths, textures, and growth patterns of the hair on everyone's heads, faces, and bodies. Blame your parents if you have any complaints or concerns about your body hair. Add it to the list.

Do you want to give yourself a new look and grow a mustache? It's not as drastic as changing your face with plastic surgery. If you don't like the look of a moustache at least you have the option of shaving it off yourself. That's much cheaper and far less messy than a re-do-it-yourself nose job.

Growing a mustache is easy. Wake up one morning and just refuse to shave your upper lip. It's foolproof. Continue your morning ritual of shaving your cheeks and chin. Or not. But that will result in a beard rather than a gloriously solo, standout 'stache. Once you've started, sit back, and watch it grow. For a week or two. It's sort of like growing a garden without the added inconvenience of feeding it manure or watering.

Sooner or later, your lip garden is going to need the edges trimmed. It's easy enough to allow your 'stache to grow naturally, trimming it every so often to a length you can live with from day to day. There's nothing wrong with sporting a natural moustache. But is it you? Or who you want to be?

Do you sport a Mohawk or a faux-hawk? A mullet or shag? Buzz cut or high and tight? Moustaches—like your choice of hairstyle—have descriptive names.

The **Walrus**—named after the animal—is a bold choice, but not without its hazards. It's bushy, hangs down over the lips, and often covers the mouth. Doesn't appeal to you? Alter this style by pulling the whiskers to each side, applying some artificial styling product and you'll be sporting the **English**. Styling it requires commitment, but it makes a striking statement.

You have a choice of upside-down U moustaches. The **Fu Manchu**—named after a fictional master criminal—is generally trimmed above the lip, with the addition of long, downward pointing ends that can be grown as long as your patience holds out. Fu's cousin is the **Pancho Villa** (named after the Mexican Revolutionary general), which is bushier in appearance. **The Horseshoe**, another popular style, is a more closely trimmed version.

The **Pencil** moustache sits high on the lip, is closely cropped, and shaved above the upper lip. The **Toothbrush** is thick, but shaved on the sides leaving the "brush" in the center. Both of these moustaches have gotten a bad

INSPECTOR CLOUSSEAU   CHE GUEVARA   THEODORE ROOSEVELT

rap: one, for being too louche; the other because it was worn by a certain psychopathic dictator. No names please.

The **Dali** is named after—you guessed it—the noted Spanish Surrealist artist, Salvador Dali. It involves close shaving and prodigious styling to achieve the lengthy, upward curving ends. Not for someone who sleeps late and wants to shower, shave, and get to work on time.

The **Handlebar**—so named due to its similarity in structure to, well, handlebars—is bushy, but trimmed with small upward-pointing (verging on curled) ends. The phrase "mustache ride" probably has more to do with actually riding on a motor-cycle or bicycle handlebars than other, bluer interpretations, or so they say. You decide.

If you're a military man, your selection of moustache style is—to say the least— extremely limited. The United States Navy insists that your 'stache shall not extend below the line of the upper lip and not go beyond a horizontal line extending across the corners of the mouth. And the length of an individual mustache hair should not exceed ½ inch in length. Eccentricities are not permitted! Good thing to know if you're thinking about enlisting.

MUSTACHE STYLES

HANDLEBAR	CHEVRON
TOOTHBRUSH	ADOLPHE MENJOU
HORSESHOE	PANCHO VILLA
FU MANCHU	CHEVRON
FRANZ JOSEPH	STRIP TEASER
WALRUS	PENCIL
	ENGLISH
	HUNGARIAN
	IMPERIAL

```
P  F  I  O  O  F  P  E  N  C  I  L  G
A  U  M  H  O  R  S  E  S  H  O  E  R
N  M  P  A  C  A  R  N  H  E  N  A  B
C  A  E  N  H  N  N  G  U  V  H  R  Q
H  N  R  D  E  Z  H  L  N  R  O  H  E
O  C  I  L  V  J  N  I  G  O  R  N  S
V  H  A  E  R  O  I  S  A  N  R  W  U
I  U  L  B  O  S  O  H  R  N  P  A  K
L  L  O  A  N  E  R  N  I  L  B  L  W
L  S  T  R  I  P  T  E  A  S  E  R  O
A  D  O  L  P  H  M  E  N  J  O  U  E
T  O  O  T  H  B  R  U  S  H  S  S  Z
```

Stylin'

Here's something to think about: the average man spends 5,000 hours or more of his life shaving. Not as much as sleeping or updating your online status, but still, it's an astonishing amount of time. And unless you decide to cultivate a full beard in addition to your mustache, you're still going to have to devote that time (and maybe more) to styling your 'stache. Be prepared to add some new tools and product (that's what my barber calls it) to your ablutions.

You can't avoid owning a comb if you have a 'stache, even if you're bald as an egg. You can use a regular hair comb, but frankly, it looks a bit ridiculous if you wield it out in public. Invest in a dainty—there's no other word for it—mustache comb. It's a bit more discreet when you neaten up after lunch. But don't—*please don't*—think you can comb your mustache at the table the way that some women reapply lipstick. If you're wearing lipstick along with a mustache, however, you may be beyond help.

Tiny, sharp scissors are handy for quick trims. Tweezers get rid of those errant whiskers that refuse to stay in line with the others. And a tiny brush comes in handy if you're pondering covering up some gray. Just be sure the color matches the rest of the 'stache.

If you're styling a more elaborate moustache, you may be concerned about keeping it up. Never fear! Moustache wax is malleable pomade applied to your moustache to hold the hairs in place, especially at those tricky extremities. Scented or unscented; colored to match your whiskers or neutral: take your pick. You can even make your own mustache wax if you wish, but that's just devoting even more time to your styling routine, so why bother? If your whiskers aren't particularly coarse (like mine), use a heat-activated styling lotion to achieve a little upward whoosh.

Feeding the 'Stache

Feeding your 'stache is unavoidable. It's one of the burdens of a hirsute upper lip. When pastries are served in the break room, you might want to avoid doughnuts topped with a dusting of confectioner's sugar. At cocktail parties, have a napkin handy if a Bloody Mary, dark stout, or draft beer is your drink of choice. When Thanksgiving rolls around, watch out for the giblet gravy. Words to the wise.

In the 19th century—the heyday of the luxuriant 'stache—when a man raised a steaming cup of coffee to his mouth the steam would melt his styling wax. In 1830, an English potter by the name of Harvey Adams introduced the first mustache cup, which featured a ledge—a

ROLLIE FINGERS   FREDERICK DOUGLASS   ROBERT GOULET   HAROLD ROSENBERG

mustache guard—across the top. Before long, potters and manufacturers everywhere were making both right and left-handed mustache cups. Following the design of mustache cups, etiquette spoons were first patented in 1868. Mustache guards that supposedly eliminated the use of a napkin have, thankfully, fallen out of fashion!

THE ACME MUSTACHE GUARD.

Solid Comfort while Eating.
No Use for Napkins.

Neat and simple, easily and quickly adjusted. Does not interfere with free use of mouth.

WORKS PERFECTLY.

Made of gold and silver plate. Can be carried in vest pocket. Every genteel person should have one. Two sizes, large and medium. Mention size when ordering. Price $2.00. Sent by mail to any address. Sold only by the

Acme Novelty Co.,
Omaha, Neb.

'MO COOKIES, PLEASE, SIR'

1 Why exert yourself? Get a roll of cookie dough, a can of icing, a squeeze tube of decorator's icing, and set of decorating tips from the grocery store.

2 Slice, bake, and cool the cookies. Spread a thin layer of icing on each cookie.

3 Test the tips that come with the decorating icing by drawing mustache shapes on a sheet of waxed paper. If you don't like the shape, wipe it off, lick your fingers, and try again. Practice makes perfect.

4 Once you've gotten the hang of it, adorn every cookie.

That's Why the Lady Wears a 'Stache

Never spit in a woman's face, unless her moustache is on fire.

This advice proves that you can find the strangest things online if your search parameters include "woman" and "mustache." Women in the office insisted that I had to include something about women and the 'stache, so here goes.

Every human being has facial hair. It's not our fault that, for the most part, males are blessed with more of it than females. But what causes a female moustache? Genetics and ethnic origins are to blame. Certain ethnic groups are more likely to develop heavier and darker facial hair than others. For most women it's a normal side effect of aging: menopause can produce an increase in facial hair. In very rare cases, *hypertrichosis*—excessive hair growth—affects both men and women. Circus sideshow performers such as Jo-Jo the Dog-Faced Boy and Lady Olga, The Bearded Lady, were afflicted by this genetic malady.

If necessary, women can shave just as their male friends do. (Just be sure you have styptic pencils and little bits of tissue handy.) In general, female facial hair is usually finer than coarse whiskers, so bleaching, tweezing (ouch!), waxing (hot, hot!), or even threading give longer lasting results. More permanent results, if desired, can be achieved with electrolysis and laser light therapies.

Let's face it: in many cultures, women with excessive facial hair have been ridiculed, ostracized, or put on exhibition. But here's an interesting cultural relic from the not-too-distant past. The Ainu of northern Japan are more hirsute than other Japanese ethnic groups. Men proudly wear profuse beards and mustaches, which are considered a sign of beauty. So much so, that married women once tattooed their lower face to mimic facial hair. Take this photo to your local tattoo parlor, if you dare!

An old Ainu woman in her native costume

FAUX 'STACHE

Are you follicularly challenged? If so, make your own faux 'stache. In a hurry? Tape it to your upper lip and enjoy your new identity. For a less-likely-to-fall-off-while-you're-dancing method, use the directions below.

1 First, choose your 'stache style. Photocopy one of the mustache templates on pages 102-104. They're about life size, more or less.

2 Get yourself some felt, craft foam, or even faux fur. Use the photocopy as a pattern to cut out your mustache.

3 Procure a 12-inch (30.5 cm) length of elastic bead thread or thin elastic. Stitch one end to the back of the mustache.

4 Adjust the length to fit around your head snugly, then stitch the free end to the other side of the mustache. Of course, you'll want to take it off your head to stitch it, unless you are very limber and ambidextrous.

Mustache Seeks Similarly Inclined

Do you sometimes wish you and your moustache had more of a social life? Thanks to your hirsute upper lip, you have all you need to join one of the many mustache clubs around the world. Here are just a few, to give you an idea of what you and your 'stache can look forward to as members.

If your moustache has that pip-pip-old boy British flair, *The Handlebar Club* may be just for you. Founded in 1947 (and still going strong), you don't have to live in the UK to be a member, but if you want to attend meetings, you'll need to trek to a pub called Windsor Castle in London on the first Friday of each month. The club offers plenty of pub time as well as competitions and charity events. In a brilliant move for an amusing competitive pairing, The Handlebar Club has reinitiated its annual darts match with The Pipe Club of London. All proceeds benefit the

ROD BECK TAREQ AZIZ EDGAR ALLAN POE CHESTER A. ARTHUR CATFISH HUNTER

Children's Liver Disease Foundation. Visit The Handlebar Club website for membership information, to purchase handlebar ties and cufflinks, and to find sage mustache-growing advice.

If flying to London, Belgium, France, Germany, or the Ukraine for meetings isn't your cup of tea, don't despair. In 1998, some mustachioed fellows in Bremerton, Washington, formed the *Whisker Club* in the tradition of the great European mustache clubs. For such a populous country, the U.S. has had some poor

First Place Moustache in the 10th Annual Beard & Mustache Competition, sponsored by The Whisker Club

Best of Show and Third Place Novice in the 10th Annual Beard & Mustache Competition, sponsored by The Whisker Club

attendance at world facial hair face-offs in the past. The club works hard to draw more Americans into the whiskery world of beard and mustache competitions. The Whisker Club's 2009 Annual Beard and Mustache Competition marked the twelfth anniversary of the event. If you're looking for something closer to home, join up with local chapters in Georgia, Texas, and Oregon, and Washington, D.C., or contact the Whisker Club to form your own chapter.

Have you ever felt the subtle sting of moustache discrimination? There's at least one proud organization that's fighting for your rights as a mustachioed citizen. *The American Mustache Institute* has vowed to regain cultural acceptance for the 'stache! Based in St. Louis, Missouri, the AMI claims the St. Louis Arch as the world's largest mustache. The AMI website posts monthly interviews online with high-profile men of the 'stache like adult film star Ron Jeremy and musician John Oates. (Why the AMI supports moving the Super Bowl from Sunday to Saturday is beyond me.) So visit their website and draw your own conclusions. But you've got to love an organization that sponsors the Robert Goulet Memorial Mustached American of the Year Award.

www.handlebarclub.co.uk
Who knew you should test your mustache curling iron with newspaper before styling your 'stache? Lesson learned.

www.whiskerclub.org
Once you've heard it, just try and get the song on the home page out of your head, I dare you!

www.americanmustacheinstitute.org
Wait for the kickass theme music to start before you click on a link.

moustachio
MAGNET

Attach

your to-do list to the refrigerator with a mustachioed magnet. Go wild: stitch one in bright orange or fluorescent green.

oil change
grocery store
get a haircut
mustache wax

1 Drive to your local craft store or wherever you buy craft supplies. You're going to need a sheet of plastic canvas, some yarn, large-eye needles, and a short length of adhesive magnetic strip for this project. If you've never, ever tried this sort of craft before, ask a friendly clerk for help in choosing the right yarn and needle.

2 Select the mustache style you want to stitch. It's best to choose a thick one; I don't suggest you use pencil thin—or a Salvador Dali–style 'stache for this project. Photocopy and enlarge one of the templates in the back of this book to the size you desire.

3 Lay the plastic canvas on the photocopy. Trace the shape. Here comes the tricky part: cut out the shape, leaving any marked squares intact.

4 If you've never stitched on plastic canvas, now's the time to go online and look for a plastic canvas tutorial. There are lots of them out there. Practice stitching on a scrap of canvas. Or just start stitching—it's easy to do and works up quickly. When your canvas shape is covered, slap on a short length of magnetic strip. Apply the 'stache to the fridge.

How in the World Do You Compliment a Moustache?

No matter what country you're from, there's a word for those whiskers on your upper lip. In English, it's either mustache or moustache: both spellings will keep you in the spelling bee. Pronounce it as you please, usually with the stress on the first syllable. Or not.

If you don't like either word, in English you can use slangy references and little sobriquets such as mouth brow, 'stache, soupstrainer, pushbroom, tash, and 'mo. Many 'mo.

Albanian = mustaqe
Arabic = شارب
Bulgarian = мустак
Croation = brkovi
Czech = knír
Dutch = snor
Estonian = viikset
Greek = μουστάκι
Hebrew = שפם
Hungarian = bajusz
Indonesian = brengos
Italian = baffi
Japanese = 口ひげ
Korean = 콧수염
Persian = سبیل
Polish = wąsy
Portuguese = bigode
Romanian = mustaţa
Russian = усы
Spanish = bigote
Swedish = mustasch
Turkish = bıyık
Ukrainian = вуса

MOUSTACHE

When I'm walking down the street, it's not uncommon for guys and girls to sneak sidelong glances and utter "awesome mustache." A couple of times they've even shouted it out of the windows of passing cars! High praise, indeed.

The web site **wordmonkey.info** translates only the word mustache but "awesome" transcends language barriers! If you're traveling and want to compliment your moustachioed brethren, you might want to use a more formal phrase. Remember to practice, practice, practice before you use it, to avoid international incidents.

Tu hermana tiene un bigote encantador.

"You have a very handsome moustache."

"Usted tiene un bigote muy guapo." (Spanish)

"У вас очень красивый усы." (Russian)

"Bạn có một ria rất đẹp trai." (Vietnamese)

"Vous avez une moustache très beau." (French)

"Hai un paio di baffi molto bello." (Italian)

"Sie haben einen sehr schönen Schnurrbart." (German)

あなたはとてもハンサムな口ひげを生やしている。(Japanese)

"Du har en mycket vacker mustasch." (Swedish)

"Máte velmi hezký knír." (Czech)

"Έχετε ένα πολύ όμορφο μουστάκι." (Greek)

"Je hebt een heel mooi snor." (Dutch)

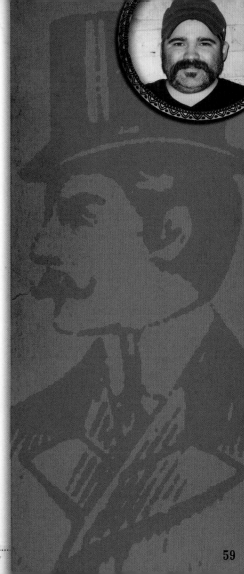

THURMAN MUNSON   GABRIEL AND CHARLES VOISIN   VIATCHEVSLAV MOLOTOV

Sell It with a 'Stache

It all began at the turn of the last century, when King Camp Gillette (yes, that's his real name) realized the value of basing a business on a disposable product. Razor blades for early safety razors needed constant sharpening just like their straight-edged forebears, so why not make them disposable? Gillette obtained a trademark registration (#0056921) for his portrait and signature on the packaging for these newfangled blades, and a marketing juggernaut was born. During World War I, Gillette was given a contract to provide his safety razors and blades as a regular part of standard-issue gear to every enlisted man or officer on his way to the Front. That explains why you don't see many photos of American military mustaches in that period.

Ettore (Hector) Boiardi opened his first restaurant, *Il Giardino d'Italia* in Cleveland, Ohio, in 1926. His customers began asking him for samples of his sauce to use at home. The sauce became so popular that in 1928 Ettore needed a factory to keep up with orders. Thus was born the sauce of Chef Bioardi, or as his American customers came to know him, Chef Boy-Ar-Dee.

Look closely at that tall can of thin chips you're nibbling through. As far as I know, that particular mustachioed character doesn't have a backstory. But another advertising character once did. Folks of a certain age will remember the Frito Bandito, the cartoon mascot for Fritos Corn Chips from 1967 to 1971. Singing a jingle to the tune of "Cielito Lindo," the bandito exclaimed, "I love Fritos Corn Chips, I love 'dem I do. I love Fritos Corn Chips, I take 'dem from you." And the chips would magically disappear. Bandito was retired

62

in 1971 under pressure from the nascent National Mexican-American Anti-Defamation Committee and others.

Cap'n Crunch's bushy mustache has been prominently featured on each and every box of his cereal since 1963. Jean LaFoote, the pencil-thin mustache-wearing Barefoot Pirate, was Cap'n Crunch's arch nemesis. Early television commercials for the product, featuring Jean and the Cap'n, were produced by Jay Ward Productions (of Rocky and Bullwinkle fame). You can see the Cap'n Crunch and Frito Bandito's commercials on **youtube.com**.

Other familiar mustaches in the world of advertising (not counting the bearded Smith Brothers) include the white-suited, goatee-sporting purveyor of all things chicken, Colonel Sanders; the imprimatur of coffee, Juan Valdez; the late, great pitchman, Billy Mays; the top hat and mustache of Mr. Monopoly; and, lest we forget, all of the celebrities who have posed with some milk on their upper lips.

1 Tomato juice. (Very scary if not wiped off immediately.)

2 Liquids with foamy heads. (Say goodbye to pub crawls.)

3 Red wine. (On the plus side: white wine doesn't stain.)

4 Gravy. (At least it's another way to reduce your cholesterol.)

5 Cigarette lighters. (Trust the voice of experience.)

6 Babies. (They're attracted to eyeglasses and mustaches.)

7 Syrup. (Thank goodness pancakes are for breakfast. There's time to take care of the mess before you go work.)

8 Shaving while half asleep. (Accidents do happen.)

9 Lipstick. (Even careful kissers sometimes get carried away.)

10 Paper shredders. (If your mustache is that close to the machine, something is wrong!)

Mustache Beware!

EAR 'STACHES

Not everyone is able to grow a mustache (you know who you are). But even those who can't, can wear dangly ones.

1 First, find some tiny moustaches. I found these plastic ones online, but I'll bet you could find them in gumball machines or craft stores as well. If you're handy with a jeweler's saw, cut some silver, copper, or acrylic sheet into mustache shapes. In a pinch, you could borrow a couple from Mr. Potato Head.

2 Drill or pierce a hole in your mustache, right near the center of the top edge.

3 Open the loop of a purchased, commercially made earwire. Slip the drilled 'stache onto the wire, and close the loop. If you're a jewelry pro, you can make your own earwires. You know how to do that.

4 Wearing matching 'stache earrings is optional. Why not be bold and wear two different 'staches at a time?

'STACHES ON THE TUBE

Mustache-less since 2001, game-show host **Alex Trebek** was once renowned for his upper lip's covering.

Ned Flanders and his hi-de-ho 'stache live in the mythical metropolis of Springfield, right next door to Homer and Marge.

Young viewers (and perhaps Mr. Bunny Rabbit) were captivated for 30 years by the uniform and distinctive gray mustache of **Captain Kangaroo**, aka Bob Keeshan.

Colorful bowties and a generous, blowsy 'stache are the trademarks for NBC's book and film critic, **Gene Shalit**.

His nose was broken during a televised brawl involving a volatile mix of guests during a 1988 interview; luckily, **Geraldo Rivera**'s moustache was unharmed.

Who among us can forget the visage of **Tom Selleck**'s mustache accessorized with a Hawaiian-print shirt and Detroit Tigers baseball cap on *Magnum P.I.*?

```
B A T S A A E R R E R K L R C
S G E N E S H A L I T N E N A
E E O E O L R A E D E L X T A
R R D R N E G K S E S N A T C
C A P T A I N K A N G A R O O
M L L E G T E A S D L L K M T
G D A S E M L R R H R E T S E
L O E B E O E O V D I X G E D
T R S T L K G L A E I T R L H
D I B E R G E E R I D R E L L
T V M L N D A H D E D E E E A
N E D F L A N D E R S B A C D
L R O A G N L L P E T E A K D
G A C R O E O R I E S K A E T
T X E C K R X A L N E R R L S
```

Some Song Lyrics and Silly 'Stache Jokes

I mustache you a question: know any good jokes or songs?

Mustaches rarely appear in song lyrics. Bob Dylan mentions one in *Visions of Johanna*; The line "My sister wears a mustache" appears in Bernstein and Sondheim's *Gee, Officer Krupke*, from West Side Story; and Mr. Margaritaville himself, Jimmy Buffett, wrote an entire song about "the Boston Blackie kind."

Jokes about mustaches must have been told in the Middle Ages or, at the very least, right after the razor was invented. Most 'stache-y jokes can't be printed here, but feel free to elaborate on the following whiskery tales as you tell them to your friends.

COLLEGE PROFESSOR: Can anyone hypothesize why a man's hair turns gray before his mustache?

STUDENT: Because his hair has a 20-year head start on his mustache.

An angry mob of cowboys is running down the street. The town barber yells, "Hey, let's hang that guy with a mustache!"

Someone else yells, "Nah, let's use a rope!"

A commuter on the subway spent much of his journey home staring at the guy sitting opposite. Before long the other guy glares back and demands to know why he is the focus of so much attention.

"I'm very sorry," begins the first man, "but if it weren't for the moustache you'd look just like my wife!"

"But I don't have a moustache!" protests the other.

And the answer to the question in the drawing is: It strains!

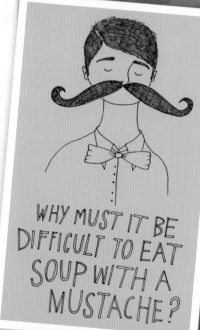

WHY MUST IT BE DIFFICULT TO EAT SOUP WITH A MUSTACHE?

The Ubiquitous Finger 'Stache

Here's the scenario: You're walking down the street. Coming from the opposite direction, you spot someone that you do not want to talk to. What do you do? Cross the street? Turn around and backtrack? Quick! Raise your index finger to your upper lip and hide behind your fake mustache!

Okay, this isn't a foolproof tactic. But it can be more effective if you had the foresight draw a mini-'stache on your finger beforehand. High fives off to the folks who contort their wrists and draw a mustache—working upside down, I might add—on their pointing digit. I've tried: it

ain't easy to do well. And if you're thinking of trying a double-palm trick without the help of a friend, more power to you!

The truly committed—or should be committed?—rush down to the local tattoo studio, whip out their debit cards, and submit their finger to the needle. It's not for the faint-of-heart or indecisive, but more power to you if you do. Can you hear the squeals of de-light from your future grandchildren?

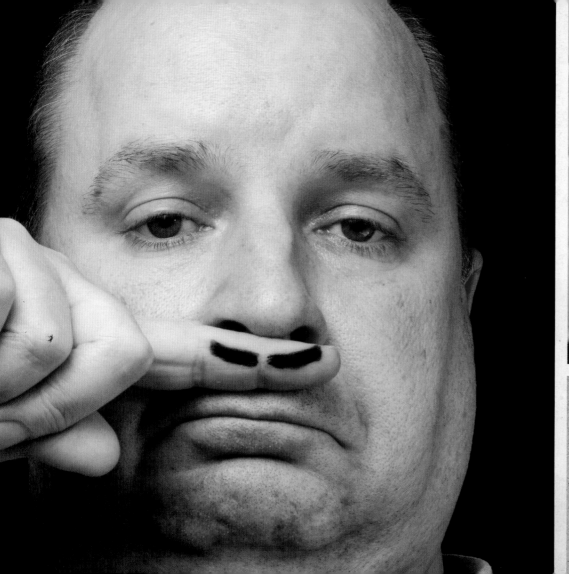

Doesn't your favorite fan deserve a finger 'stache to tote along to a sporting event? How about taking one to the next interminable staff meeting? It's a sure way to stand out from the crowd.

1. Purchase a giant foam finger (that's a technical term, I believe) at your local foam finger store. I found this one online.

2. Grab your choice of acrylic paint and a brush. Decide which mustache style suits your foam finger best. Paint one on there. (If you're doing this at the office, you can use that white stuff you use to cover your mistakes with. It's a bit more time-consuming, but you're doing it at work, aren't you?)

3. Allow the paint or white stuff to dry completely before you start waving your finger around!

Our Whiskered Animal Friends

Humans don't have a monopoly on fuzzy upper lips. Animals have mustaches, too! Our mustached neighbors in the animal kingdom walk the earth, swim the seas, and soar through our skies, proudly preening the 'staches Mother Nature gave them.

The emperor tamarin—a monkey found in the treetops of South American tropical rain forests— wears a drooping imperial mustache. Named for their resemblance to the last German emperor and King of Prussia, Wilhelm II, these regal monkeys grow natural mustaches that outshine those of even the most dedicated mustache groomers.

Pinnipeds—fin-footed marine mammals like seals, sea lions, and walruses—sport some great facial hair. Bush-lipped and tubby, walruses wear wonderful mustaches that call to mind former U.S. president, William Howard Taft. Harbor seals (and possibly other pinnipeds) use their whiskers for underwater hunting by sensing hydrodynamic trails left by swimming fish. If the U.S. Navy didn't have such stringent mustache guidelines, perhaps they could train some of their members to use their whiskers for some underwater reconnaissance.

Tigers, panthers, and other big cats put their wispy whiskers to use in sensing their surroundings, just like our domestic kitties. Rooted in facial areas packed with nerves, a cat's whiskers, or "tactile hairs," are so sensitive that felines can use them to feel direction changes in the slightest breeze! Those whiskery mustaches also serve to make our kitties irresistibly adorable.

Even a few of our non-mammalian friends have their own forms of mustache. The Inca tern, a beautiful South American seabird, has a curling, white feather mustache. And don't forget the catfish! Its mustache-like appendages—called barbels—are tactile organs that house the fish's taste buds. And they may also have inspired the funk rock band name, Catfish Mustache.

So next time you're thinking of a new style of mustache to sport, try looking to our animal cousins for ideas. Your mustache won't be made from feathers or help you navigate, but with a little inspiration from nature, it could sure be wild!

Mustaches in the Library

Quickly now, how many authors can you think of who have a mustache? Off the top of my head I can come up with Balzac, E.M. Forster, Flaubert, Hemingway, Proust, and Sonny Bono. (Yes, Sonny Bono. *Sonny Bono and The Beat Goes On* was his autobiography.) See how handy a degree in English is? You will surely recognize the two mustachioed American authors on this page.

Until I started researching this book, I'd never thought much about mustaches and the written word before. There's not too much out there, except a short story by Nikolai Gogol entitled "The Nose." But was there a mustache under it?

ENGELBERT HUMPERDINCK   DR. ZIN

Guy de Maupassant—you read his story "The Necklace" in high school—paid homage to the moustache in his cleverly titled story, "The Mustache." In the story, Jeanne writes a letter to Lucy with the following whiskers of wisdom:

"In fact, a man without a mustache is no longer a man."

"But a mustache, oh, a mustache is indispensable to a manly face."

"No, you would never believe how these little hair bristles on the upper lip are a relief to the eye and good in other ways."

"There is no love without a moustache."

And then Jeanne proceeds to describe to Lucy the intoxicating tickle of the moustache on the face, neck, and lips! She knows whereof she speaks!

You can find variations on the "man without a moustache" theme in common maxims from around the globe. In England, "a man without a mustache is like a cup of tea without sugar"; in Italy, "a kiss without a moustache is like beef without mustard"; and the French compare it to an egg without salt. I'll bet you can come up with even bawdier versions if you put your mind to it. I'm pretty sure de Maupassant isn't accurately quoted in the photo of that park bench, although I agree with the sentiment.

POLITICALLY INCLINED MUSTACHES

California Congressman **Henry Waxman**'s nickname is "Mustache of Justice".

Kofi Annan of Ghana was the seventh Secretary-General of the United Nations.

Referred to by American Communists in the 1930s as Uncle Joe, **Joseph Stalin**'s bushy mustache was his trademark.

The president of Mexico from 2000 to 2006, **Vincente Fox** sported a suave 'stache.

The rough-riding **Theodore Roosevelt** was the 26th president of the United States.

G. Gordon Liddy, one of the White House plumbers (ca. 1972), sported a formidable brushy mustache.

Vladimir Lenin and his pencil-thin moustache are eternally entombed in Red Square.

THEODORE ROOSEVELT

```
C  I  N  F  O  M  L  G  S  P  E  T  G  N  D  X  D
R  H  R  R  D  V  A  E  D  O  M  N  S  H  O  E  I
T  I  M  Y  E  L  O  F  R  L  E  C  I  V  R  N  T
H  M  I  C  H  A  E  L  C  H  E  R  T  O  F  F  O
R  G  G  O  R  D  O  N  L  I  D  D  Y  A  L  F  H
N  N  K  O  F  I  A  N  N  A  N  N  A  O  A  J  D
E  M  O  E  G  M  O  A  L  I  N  O  L  V  V  N  F
Y  F  X  E  V  I  C  E  N  T  E  F  O  X  S  E  O
R  N  N  R  O  R  E  O  E  W  F  F  H  A  D  E  F
O  R  N  N  T  L  E  D  R  W  A  S  S  C  N  I  N
O  O  J  O  S  E  P  H  S  T  A  L  I  N  A  N  R
S  D  A  R  X  N  O  D  E  I  A  N  N  S  O  C  E
T  I  L  R  I  I  H  O  E  I  L  J  N  Y  N  N  S
O  S  M  H  E  N  R  Y  W  A  X  M  A  N  D  L  T
D  S  K  L  H  R  D  L  F  A  D  A  L  O  A  A  O
O  Y  L  N  X  Y  N  I  D  H  P  O  A  I  F  O  X
T  H  E  O  D  O  R  E  R  O  O  S  E  V  E  L  T
```

Mustaches for a Better World

Snidely Whiplash may be a classic villain-with-a-mustache, but bad guys aren't the only ones twirling mustaches! Men and women around the world are fighting the good fight with facial hair by raising money for charitable initiatives. Mustache marathons plus fun pageant parties result in a boost for the funded charities.

The Movember Foundation invented the "mustache month" for charity growing. During the month of November, participants grow mustaches to raise money for men's health awareness initiatives focusing on depression and prostate cancer. At the end of November, Movember chapters around the world host sensational costume galas, Mo Office Parties, and wild Mo Town Parties in at least seven countries. There are around six categories for fame and glory to be had at the worldwide galas. The puniest mustache gets The Lame Mo award while the rockin'est takes The International Man of Movember title. They didn't forget the ladies, either! The best-dressed Mo Sista becomes Miss Movember, a title of no small prestige. **www.us.movember.com**

If you want to do good in the UK, you can always grow a tache and raise cash with TacheBack. Tache Teams and individuals grow sponsored mustaches through the month of September to raise money for Everyman, a leading British campaign for

SEAN CONNERY   FREDDIE MERCURY   GARRY MADDOX   CHARLES BRONSON testicular and prostate cancer research. Crazy TacheBack Challenges and strategies are announced on their website throughout September. Participants put on their most gruesome grimaces for the camera to show off their budding 'staches in week four of the competition. **www.tacheback.com**

Mustaches for Kids is a volunteer organization that uses mustached fundraisers to support children's charities. Founded for giving and fun in Los Angeles, California, in 1999, this initiative has grown steadily through the careful addition of satellite chapters. They've supported some great organizations, including the Make-A-Wish Foundation, the Children's Hospital of New Orleans, and San Francisco's

Legal Services for Children. Growing season runs during the four weeks from Thanksgiving to Christmas. If you want to participate, make sure you check out the Mustaches for Kids bylaws, and grow accordingly. At the end of the season, chapters host a super-campy Mustache Competition complete with lineup and mustache-augmenting costumes. In the end, there can be only one mustache, and it will be declared the sweetest. **www.mustachesforkids.org**

Join the brave men and artificially-mustachioed women who've given the gift of 'stache. Surely you can spare a month of your life for doing good and getting to twirl your own mustache in the bargain.

WE WANT YOU

MOVEMBER enlist now...

Better than dancing on the table or wearing the proverbial lampshade on the head, these 'staches give you something to hide behind as you party on.

1 You'll need to buy sheets of craft foam for waterproof mustaches, as well as drinking glasses with attached straws or some bendable straws. That's it.

2 Duplicate any one of the mustaches in the back of this book and use it as a template to cut out a mustache.

3 Carefully poke a hole in the mustache with a pair of sharp scissors or use a small hole punch if you have one. The foam will stretch a bit as you slip it onto the straw.

4 Party on behind the 'stache. Cheers!

The Graffiti 'Stache

Graffiti isn't a new phenomenon: there's graffiti in the ruins of Pompeii (and maybe in the caves of Lascaux for all I know). Graffiti—in all its glory—can be found around the world. Aside from gang signs and other tags, what's the most popular graffiti motif? Why it's the mustache! The moustache is timeless and universal.

So, why is tagging a photo or a drawing with a mustache everyone's hands-down favorite? Here's the simple truth: you don't have to be an art-school graduate to draw the simple 'stache. All you have to do is pencil in a pair of straight lines or scribble a small rectangle under a nose and, *voilà—le moustache!* A six-year-old can do it. With her eyes closed, I'll bet.

Admit it: at some point in your life, haven't you been overcome with the urge to scrawl a mous-

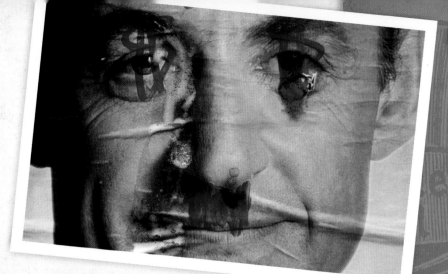

tache onto something? Perhaps the photos of your ex you should have thrown out three years ago, or your arch nemesis in the high school yearbook? Sure you have. Everyone has. It's therapeutic!

However, you should draw the line at adorning campaign posters and billboards with 'staches, just in principle. Besides, the metal ladders on those tall billboards are scary things to climb. Not that I would know, of course. And I'd urge you to really think twice about using a can of spray paint on the side of a building, unless you can run very fast. Or have a hankering to be handcuffed by a police officer with a Fu Manchu mustache. But that's another issue altogether.

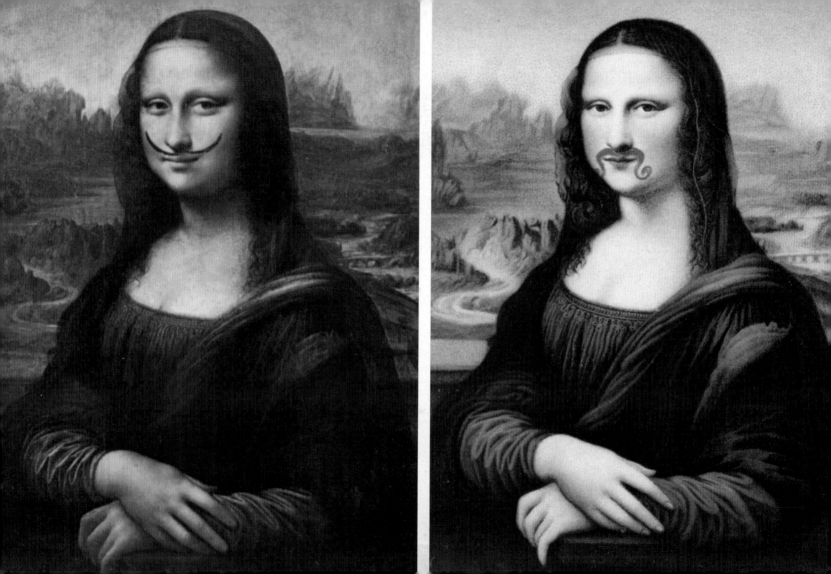

May I

Tickle
Your
Fancy?

Kiss Off!

send someone A 'STACHE

The recipient of one of these cards won't forget who sent it—ever.

1. Purchase some blank greeting cards, stick-on lettering, and small amounts of fabric or felt. You probably have some glue you can use at home. I used a rubber stamp of pursed lips on my cards. If you can't find a rubber stamp to use, put on some lipstick and pucker up!

2. Photocopy one of the templates in the back of this book to use as a pattern. Cut a mustache shape out of your fabric.

3. Glue the 'stache on a blank card and embellish the card as you wish.

4. Feel free to use the sentiments I came up with or make up your own.

Imaginary 'Staches

When was the last time you sat in a school cafeteria filled with 10-year-olds? How about an all-night dining establishment at 3:30 a.m. after an evening of carousing with your homeboys? In either setting, chances are someone has picked up a French fry, held it just below his (or her) nose, and was rewarded with the sound of laughter, if not outright guffaws of glee.

Welcome to the wonderful world of imaginary 'staches. You can also refer to them as conceptual moustaches—just like I do—if you've taken at least one art history class or know someone who has.

An imaginary/conceptual mustache isn't functional; it's temporary, of-the-moment, or ephemeral. You have to hold it in place with at least one hand

or uncomfortably contort your upper lip. Now, I'm not saying that you can't use some super-duper glue to adhere it to your upper lip, but I wouldn't advise your doing so unless your health insurance covers such ill-advised procedures. An imaginary 'stache exists in the mind—until inspiration strikes in the break room or sitting at the local watering hole.

Let's face facts: clowning around at the table isn't looked kindly on by Miss Manners, your mother, or most fourth-grade teachers. What you do in the privacy of your own home is your business. At 3:45 a.m. who cares?

Crinkle-cut potatoes make credible mustaches (ketchup is optional and messy). So do puffed artificial cheese snacks held aloft on a fork. The leafy ends of celery? Quick: How many other edible 'staches can you come up with? A good many, I'll bet.

Once you start thinking about it, there are all sorts of conceptual 'staches you can create. Use some interlocking plastic blocks (you know the ones) to build a mustache. Look at the obvious possibility your sushi takeout tray offers. Brushes? Candies? Office supplies! Oh, the places you will go with your imaginary mo'.

LEIGH COUNTY FAIR

MUSTACHE GROWING

CHAMPION

august 26th - 1981

Celebrate with a 'STACHE

HAPPY

MOUSTACHE

1 Get yourself a cake mix, a couple of cans of vanilla icing, and a bag of shredded coconut. If coconut icing doesn't appeal to you, perhaps you'd prefer darker whiskers. Use chocolate icing, but omit the coconut unless you're aiming for an older gentleman's look.

2 Bake the cake in a 13 x 9-inch pan. Allow the cake to cool completely before cutting it into a mustache shape. Eat the leftover cake as you go—you deserve it. Carefully slide the cake onto a flat surface such as covered cardboard or the backside of cookie sheet.

3 Ice the cake, smoothing out the icing as you go. Sprinkle the cake liberally with coconut. Or not.

99

VERSATILE MUSTACHE
MASQUES

This dual-duty masque is handy if you can't sleep on airplanes or need a disguise. Take care choosing which version to wear on overnight flights—you don't want to upset the Federal Air Marshal sitting next to you.

1 Purchase some craft felt and ribbon.

2 Enlarge and photocopy the template on page 105. Use the photocopy as a template and cut two identical shapes out of felt.

3 Pin the two shapes together, catching a length of ribbon at either side. Stitch the shapes together.

4 Tie the ribbons around your head and nighty-night! If your mask is for deception, carefully snip out the eyeholes with sharp scissors before you put it on.

Templates

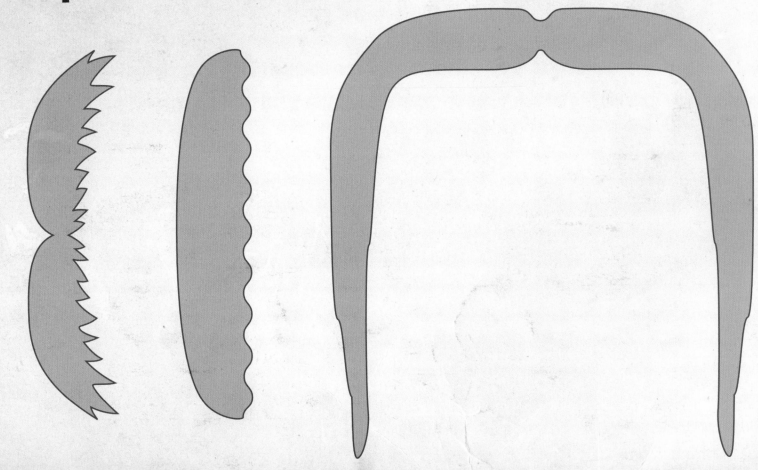

Templates

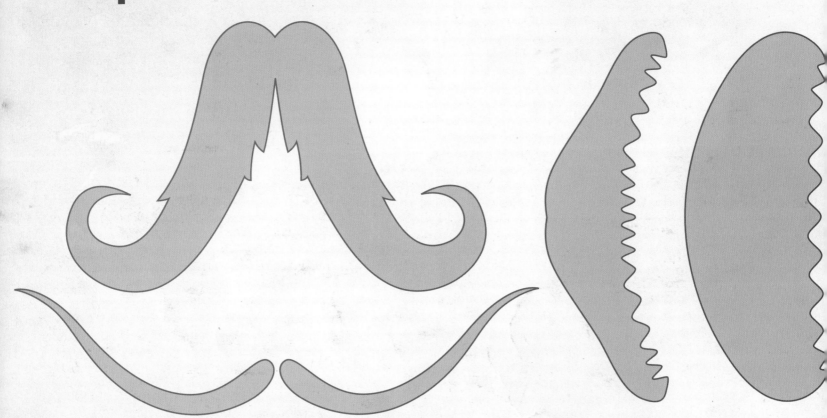

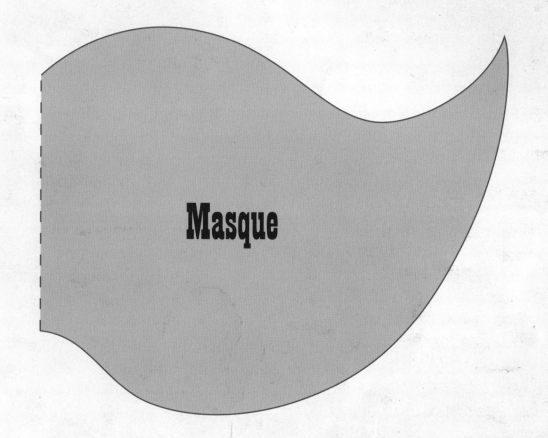

Masque

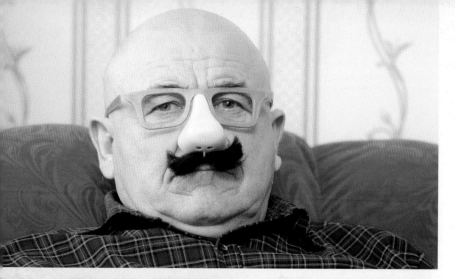

Acknowledgments

A very special thank you goes to Marthe who patiently listened to a late-night, bright idea and to Amanda, Kristi, and Shannon who helped develop content in the early stages.

Amanda, Matt, Beth, and Frank left their desks and shed their dignity to don a variety of 'staches. You guys are the best.

A special thank you to Beth the baker of 'stache-y goodies—it didn't take long for that cake to disappear, did it?

I stand in awe of Bradley, whose one-o'clock shadow provided a luxuriant handlebar in record time.

Kudos to Travis, Shannon, and Chris—you guys made it all look good.

Tom Boza urged me to go ahead and let it grow. So, thanks to him for 20 years of haircuts and 'stache stylin'.

Image Credits

Find It Here

Meet the Moustache

If you've flipped through the pages, you're probably wondering: Who is that 'stached man in the upper right hand corner? Bradley Norris' one-o'clock shadow appeared around age 12—in the sixth grade. His military dad made him shave each and every day (sometimes twice!), so he didn't display his miraculous ability to grow a beard or 'stache to the world until he ventured off to college. It took him approximately three months (!) to achieve the supreme handlebar-ness pictured at right.

JOHN BOLTON   ERROL FLYNN   ROSCOE ORMAN   STEVE PREFONTAINE   HULK HOGAN

TED NUGENT   JOE NAMATH   MIKE DITKA   SARAH SILVERMAN   LECH WALESA